PIM AND THE GOOD NEIGHBOR

BY JOSELYNE KUDERHA

Typesetting by Roy Kamau
www.royKcreative.com

Illustrated by Sudipta Basu

Hope: Mommy, I'm home!

Mom: Hi Hope! how was school today?

Hope: School was fine, mommy. We had a new girl today in our class.

Mom: How lovely dear, what is her name?

Hope: Her name is Rachel, but I was sad that some kids were making fun of her red hair during recess. I wanted to help her, but I didn't know what to do.

Mom: Oh no, come sit down, hun. I have a story to tell you.

Mom: But first, tell me, how can you be a good neighbor?

Hope: I can be a good neighbor by being kind and helpful to others, right, mom?

Mom: Yes, Hope, you are right. Being kind and helpful to your neighbors is very important. Now, let me tell you a story about Pim and the Good Neighbor.

Hope: Oh, yay! I can't wait to hear this story.

Long ago, in the bustling city of Nameria,
there lived a cheerful boy named Pim.

Now, Pim was from one of the four tribes in this city, the yellow tribe, who were Known for their infectious joy and laughter.

One day, as Pim happily sKipped to buy his favorite snacKs, he encountered some robbers on his path.

They attacked Pim, taking his money and leaving him wounded.

His bright smile vanished as he cried out for help as he was too wounded to walk.

Fortunately, a man from the red clan strolling on the same path, spotted Pim injured on the ground. The red clan was Known for their Kind hearts, so surely, he would have helped Pim.

"Oh no!" he exclaimed.

"Please help me!" Pim yelled.

Fearful of the robbers, the man quickly ran to the other side, leaving Pim helpless.

Later, a man from the purple clan walked by. The purple clan was friendly, and Pim hoped for help.

"Please help," Pim cried out. "They took all my money and left me hurt."

Despite wanting to help, the man from the purple clan walked away, leaving Pim helpless and alone.

All this made Pim sad, but then a man
from the green clan saw him and started
running toward him.

But Pim felt afraid because the green clan
was Known for being greedy and mean.

To Pim's surprise, the man from the green clan chose to help him by rushing him to the nearest clinic.

The man paid for Pim's wounds to be treated and even prepared a hot bowl of soup for Pim.

Surely, Pim thought aloud, "why are you doing all of this?"

The man from the green clan then said, "As a good neighbor, you must do unto others what you want them to do unto you."

Mom: What's touching about this story is that Kindness can come from anyone.

Mom: The red and purple clans might have seemed more likely to help, but in the end, someone unlikely was the true helper.

Mom: So, honey, how can you be a good neighbor?

Hope: I can help Rachel when others pick on her and show kindness to everyone else.

Mom: That's right. Do unto others what you want them to do unto to you.

Hope: Okay, Mommy, I will. (Kisses Mommy's cheek).

Father, help my dear child to be a light and a true example of your love for their classmates and all those around them.

In Jesus' Name, Amen.

Author's Note:

Pim's story is inspired by the Good Samaritan in Luke 10:25-37. I encourage you to read this parable together and revisit Pim's story to teach your children to be kind and loving neighbors throughout their lives.

www.ingramcontent.com/pod-product-compliance
Lightning Source LLC
Chambersburg PA
CBHW041036120726

48006CB00005B/1211